Momentous Materials

Cotton

by Dalton Rains

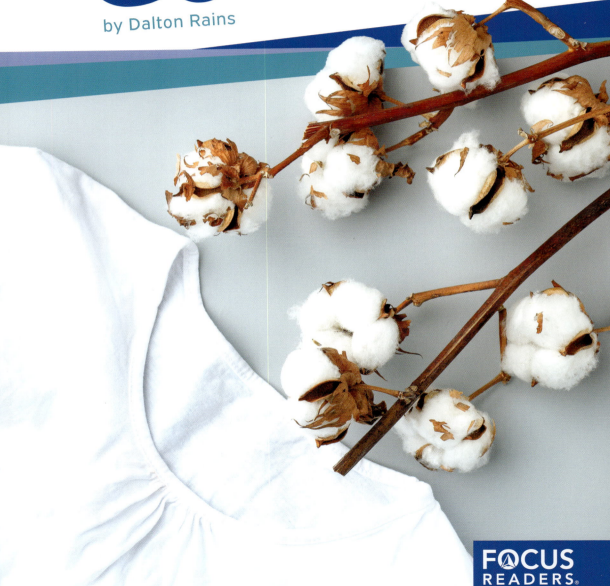

FOCUS READERS
BEACON

www.focusreaders.com

Copyright © 2024 by Focus Readers®, Mendota Heights, MN 55120. All rights reserved. No part of this book may be reproduced or utilized in any form or by any means without written permission from the publisher.

Focus Readers is distributed by North Star Editions:
sales@northstareditions.com | 888-417-0195

Produced for Focus Readers by Red Line Editorial.

Photographs ©: Shutterstock Images, cover, 1, 4, 7, 8, 11, 14–15, 16, 19, 20, 22, 25, 27, 29; Historical Views/agefotostock/Alamy, 12

Library of Congress Cataloging-in-Publication Data
Names: Rains, Dalton, author.
Title: Cotton / by Dalton Rains.
Description: Mendota Heights, MN : Focus Readers, [2024] | Series: Momentous materials | Includes bibliographical references and index. | Audience: Grades 2-3
Identifiers: LCCN 2023030846 (print) | LCCN 2023030847 (ebook) | ISBN 9798889980315 (hardcover) | ISBN 9798889980742 (paperback) | ISBN 9798889981565 (ebook pdf) | ISBN 9798889981176 (hosted ebook)
Subjects: LCSH: Cotton--Juvenile literature. | Cotton textile industry--History--Juvenile literature. | Cotton machinery--Juvenile literature. | Cotton fabrics--Juvenile literature.
Classification: LCC TS1542 .R35 2024 (print) | LCC TS1542 (ebook) | DDC 633.5/109--dc23/eng/20230701
LC record available at https://lccn.loc.gov/2023030846
LC ebook record available at https://lccn.loc.gov/2023030847

Printed in the United States of America
Mankato, MN
012024

About the Author

Dalton Rains is a writer and editor from Saint Paul, Minnesota.

Table of Contents

CHAPTER 1
Cozy Morning 5

CHAPTER 2
History of Cotton 9

THAT'S AMAZING!
Cottonseed Oil 14

CHAPTER 3
Modern Methods 17

CHAPTER 4
Uses of Cotton 23

Focus on Cotton • 28
Glossary • 30
To Learn More • 31
Index • 32

Chapter 1

Cozy Morning

A girl wakes up on a chilly winter morning. She opens her dresser. She pulls out a thick cotton sweater. She also grabs a pair of cotton sweatpants. These clothes keep her nice and warm.

 Cotton is used to make many different kinds of clothing.

Next, the girl goes to the kitchen. Her mother is making herself coffee. She puts the coffee grounds in a filter. The filter is made with cotton.

After breakfast, the girl and her mother head to the living room. Together, they start a fire in the

Did You Know?

There are several different kinds of cotton. Some are white. Others are brown, red, or green.

 Cotton blankets keep people warm by trapping body heat.

fireplace. The girl curls up with a cotton blanket. Then, she picks up her favorite book. The pages are held together with cotton. On this cozy morning, cotton is all around.

Chapter 2

History of Cotton

Cotton comes from a plant. It grows in warm parts of the world. Humans have been using cotton for many years. By 4000 BCE, several ancient peoples were growing it. They **wove** cotton to make fabrics.

 The fluffy white material is the cotton plant's fruit. People cannot eat it, though.

9

Some of these ancient peoples lived in the Americas. Others lived in Asia and North Africa.

Around 300 BCE, people brought cotton to Europe. Cotton was softer than most other fabrics. However, few people could afford it.

In the late 1400s, Europeans started taking over the Americas. They saw lots of wild cotton. Soon, they began growing the plant on farms. In the 1600s, they started using enslaved workers.

 After the cotton gin was invented, people could produce far more cotton than before.

Cotton plants are filled with seeds. The seeds had to be removed by hand. This process took a long time. But in 1793, the cotton gin was invented. This machine could remove the seeds quickly.

 White farm owners enslaved Black people and forced them to work in awful conditions.

Cotton became cheaper. As a result, more people wanted to buy it. However, growing cotton still took lots of work. So, farm owners enslaved more people. Farm owners sent the cotton to

textile mills. These factories turned the cotton into fabrics.

Slavery ended in 1865. After that, US farms continued to grow lots of cotton. But other countries started growing even more. By the 2020s, India and China were the world's leaders.

Did You Know?

More than 27 million tons (24.5 million metric tons) of cotton is produced every year.

THAT'S AMAZING!

Cottonseed Oil

People use cotton for more than just fabric. It can also be used to make cottonseed oil. Factories put this oil into certain foods. Many kinds of potato chips and crackers include cottonseed oil. It helps these foods last longer. Some restaurants use cottonseed oil, too. They use it to fry foods.

Cottonseed oil can also be found in other products. For instance, it is in many soaps. And some people put it in their hair. The oil keeps hair from getting dry.

Cottonseed oil can help stop people's skin from drying out.

Chapter 3

Modern Methods

Today, farmers use machines to grow and **harvest** cotton. First, they plant seeds. Months later, green pods start to appear on the plants. These pods are called cotton bolls. **Fibers** grow inside.

Machines help farmers harvest thousands of pounds of cotton per day.

Then, heat from the sun causes the fibers to expand. The bolls split open. Fluffy cotton bursts out.

After harvesting the cotton, farmers use machines to pack it into large cubes. Next, other machines dry the cotton. Then, machines remove dirt, stems, and leaves. Finally, strands of cotton are

Did You Know?

Cotton plants take five to six months to grow.

 Cubes of cotton are called modules. Farmers often cover modules to keep them dry.

pulled through another machine.

This process removes the seeds.

The cotton fiber is now called lint.

The lint is then formed into **bales**.

 Today, there are thousands of textile mills in the United States.

The bales are very large. Each one can weigh 500 pounds (227 kg).

The bales are then sent to textile mills. First, each bale goes through a carding machine. This machine works like a comb. It cleans and straightens the fibers. It turns the fiber into a soft rope called a sliver. A machine spins the sliver many times. This process twists the sliver into yarn. Then, machines called looms weave the yarn into fabric.

　　After that, the woven fabric moves to finishing plants. Here, machines add **dye**. This gives the cotton its color. Then it can be used in clothing or other products.

Chapter 4

Uses of Cotton

Cotton has a wide variety of uses. Many people wear clothing made of cotton. There are several different kinds of cotton fabric. Each has a distinct **texture**. Denim is rough. Flannel is soft.

 Cotton is a popular fabric because it is soft and comfortable.

Velvet is even softer. To make each type of fabric, machines use different weaving patterns. They also treat each fabric with different **chemicals**.

Cotton has other uses around the house. For instance, most towels and washcloths are made from cotton. Many bedspreads and

One bale of cotton is enough to make 1,200 shirts.

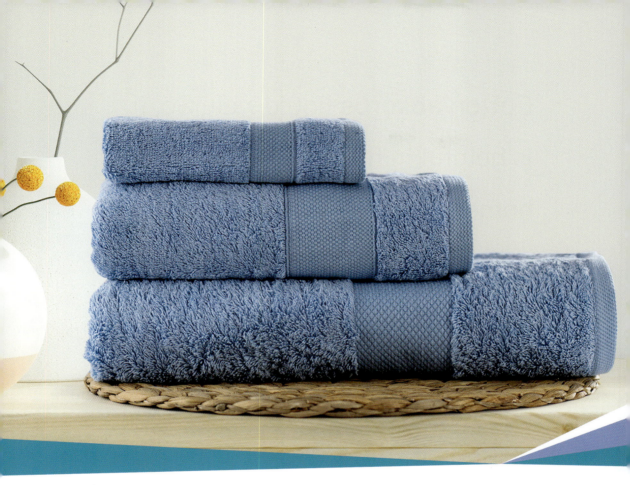

 Cotton easily soaks up water, so it's a good material for towels.

pillowcases use cotton. Window shades often use cotton, too.

Medical products are another important way people use cotton.

Cotton **absorbs** liquid well. So, it is helpful in hospitals and nursing homes. Bandages are often made with cotton. So are diapers and baby wipes.

Cotton has other surprising uses. For instance, cotton can be used for book binding. This helps keep pages together. Some kinds of paper also include cotton. Dollar bills are made with the material. It protects the bills from liquid. Cotton is also used for outdoor

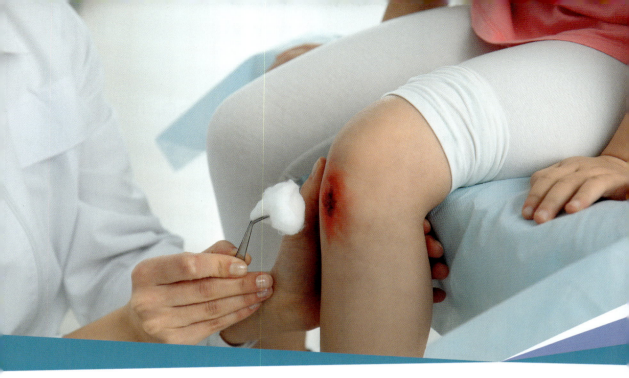

 Cotton can help clean scrapes and other injuries.

products. Examples include tents and fishing nets.

Cotton products are found all over the world. Many people use it every day. It is one of the most important materials on Earth.

FOCUS ON
Cotton

Write your answers on a separate piece of paper.

1. Write a paragraph describing the main ideas of Chapter 2.

2. What is your favorite way to use cotton in your daily life? Why?

3. Which machine takes the seeds out of cotton?
    - **A.** carding machine
    - **B.** cotton gin
    - **C.** loom

4. Why is cotton helpful in hospitals?
    - **A.** It looks stylish.
    - **B.** It soaks up blood.
    - **C.** It falls off easily.

5. What does **ancient** mean in this book?

*Humans have been using cotton for many years. By 4000 BCE, several **ancient** peoples were growing it.*

- **A.** from long ago
- **B.** good at farming
- **C.** hidden or unusual

6. What does **distinct** mean in this book?

*Each has a **distinct** texture. Denim is rough. Flannel is soft. Velvet is even softer.*

- **A.** rough or hard to the touch
- **B.** similar to something else
- **C.** not like something else

Answer key on page 32.

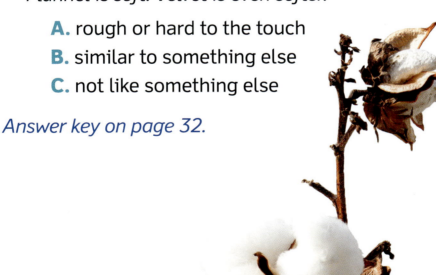

Glossary

absorbs
Soaks up a liquid.

bales
Large bundles of a material.

chemicals
Specific kinds of matter. Some chemicals can be harmful, and some can be helpful.

dye
Something that is added to a material to give it a different color.

fibers
Threads or structures that look like threads.

harvest
To gather crops.

textile mills
Factories that make cloth, usually by knitting or weaving.

texture
The feeling of something.

wove
Created fabric by lacing threads together.

To Learn More

BOOKS

Kukla, Lauren. *Designing with Textiles: DIY Fabric & Fiber Projects*. Minneapolis: Abdo Publishing, 2023.

Pearson, Yvonne. *How Do We Classify Materials?* North Mankato, MN: Capstone Press, 2022.

Smith, Elliott. *The Slave Trade: Black Lives and the Drive for Profit*. Minneapolis: Lerner Publications, 2022.

NOTE TO EDUCATORS

Visit **www.focusreaders.com** to find lesson plans, activities, links, and other resources related to this title.

Index

A
Americas, 10
ancient peoples, 9–10

B
bales, 19–20, 24
bolls, 17–18

C
carding machine, 21
China, 13
clothing, 5, 21, 23
cotton gin, 11
cottonseed oil, 14

D
dye, 21

E
Europe, 10

F
finishing plants, 21

H
harvesting, 17–18

I
India, 13

M
medical products, 25–26

N
North Africa, 10

S
seeds, 11, 17, 19
slavery, 10, 12–13

T
textile mills, 12–13, 20–21
texture, 23

W
weaving, 9, 21, 24

Answer Key: **1.** Answers will vary; **2.** Answers will vary; **3.** B; **4.** B; **5.** A; **6.** C